someone's mother

A Collection of Poetry

Jenny Bravo

Copyright © 2024 by Jenny Bravo

All rights reserved.

No part of this book may be reproduced in any form or by any electronic or mechanical means, including information storage and retrieval systems, without written permission from the author, except for the use of brief quotations in a book review.

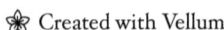 Created with Vellum

For Belle

Love, Mama

Thank you for being mine

contents

Introduction	ix
Mornings	1
i.	2
The Newborn Stage Is A Fever Dream	3
ii.	4
I Made You	5
What Did We Get Ourselves Into?	6
Is She A Good Baby?	8
iii.	10
C-Section Scars	11
If You Are Awake Right Now	12
iv.	14
Maternity Leave	15
Time Is A Thief	16
Belle	19
v.	20
My Mother Is Magic	21
vi.	22
You Look Great, Mama!	23
vii.	24
Let Me Never Forget	25
viii.	26
Someone's Mother	27
ix.	28
Mother Feelings	29
An Anxious Mother	30
x.	32
Club Baby	33
xi.	34
Bounce Back	35
The World I Want To Show You	36
Actually, I Can Wait	37
xii.	38

My Husband Is A Father Now	39
xiii.	40
Firsts and Lasts	41
xiv.	42
I Miss This Already	43
Sisters	44
xv.	46
Boring Is Beautiful	47
xvi.	48
She Looks Just Like You!	49
xvii.	50
Everything Changes	51
I Wish You Were Here To Meet Her	52
My Heart Is A Person Now	54
What I'd Give Up	55
Big Family	56
We Grow Together	58
xviii.	60
I Dreamed New Dreams	61
xix.	62
Mom Guilt (Baby Edition)	63
Father Figures	64
Unoriginal	67
xx.	68
I Keep You	69
xxi.	70
Sensations	71
Fur Baby	72
xxii.	74
Legacy	75
Nights	76
Also by Jenny Bravo	77
Acknowledgments	79
About the Author	81

introduction

There is only one time in my life when I considered myself a poet. I was probably twelve-years-old and I wore a beret on my head that I labeled my "poetry cap." This little, awkward version of myself decided that in order to make great art, I needed to look the part. (Which apparently, was French.)

Turns out all I needed was a baby.

I wrote and published my first novel in 2015. I have always thought of myself as a fiction writer. I still do. And yet, when I had a baby, real life became so much more interesting. And lyrical, I suppose.

I wrote these poems in the middle of the night when my daughter didn't want to be out of my arms. I wrote them from the five minutes I got in the bathtub before she wanted to nurse again. I wrote them from contact naps, from maternity leave, through a rollercoaster of emotions.

This book is for mothers. Ones who are currently in the trenches of newborn life as well as those who are looking back at them with foggy memories. You're incredible. And I hope you know that.

mornings

Good morning, little one.

I unswaddle you.

Big stretchy arms.

I reach for you, lift you up.

Arching in a crescent moon.

I kiss your face, singsong hello.

Babbles and big giant smiles.

Mornings were never quite

as good before there was you.

i.

I felt complete
before you
but I feel
a m p l i f i e d
with you

the newborn stage is a fever dream

The newborn stage is 8 weeks of *what is going on?* We need more mylicon drops! It's your turn. When was the last time you took a shower? Can we come see the baby? Update: she doesn't like her crib anymore. Update: she doesn't like her bassinet anymore. Help, it's going too slowly! Help, it's going too fast! My eyes have never been heavier. I've never been so tired in my whole life. How's she sleeping? How are you sleeping, mama? *Mama. Mama. She needs her mama.* Look at all that hair! Have you tried the rocking chair? It won't always be like this. Oh no, it won't always be like this.

ii.

first it was he and i

two fools in love

with a whole lot of free time

now we have you

and we don't know what we would do

without your perfect little smile

i made you

God made woman
from a rib torn out of man
And I made you from

    twenty-three years of heavy menstrual cramps
    epsom salt baths and hot water bottles
    OBGYN appointments with speculums and cold hands
    ovulation strips, tracking apps, and pregnancy tests
    pickle chips and no-pulp orange juice
    instagram research and anxious texts to mom friends
    late night prayers after crazy nightmare dreams
    tears that flowed after butchered cookie recipes
    nine months of watching us change and grow
    thirty-eight hours laboring in a dark hospital room
    one hour of surgery under stark white operating lights
    a moment of bliss when I saw you for the very first time

And it was (mostly) so very good

what did we get ourselves into?

Our first night at home

We settle into our new normal

Children stepping into

Our parents' too-big shoes

We think we know her already

like she's a puzzle

we have finished solving

and then

    she surprises us

Once quiet, now screaming

Once sleepy, now alarmed

Once satiated, now ravenous

Husband and I face each other
Worried
  Scared
    Overwhelmed
      Exhausted
And he asks the question we both think
"What did we get ourselves into?"

What did we get ourselves into?
Long, endless nights of crying
Swaddling and unswaddling
Diaper changes after unexpected blowouts
Constant changes in routines that don't stick

What did we get ourselves into?
Perfect mornings with a happy, smiling baby
Warm evenings with our cuddly, clean girl
Baby shampoo and baby moisturizer
Small, soft onesies and sweet baby blankets

We have gotten ourselves into parenthood
We have gotten ourselves into life

is she a good baby?

She is good when

she wakes every hour

her cry slicing

through the quiet night

She is good when

she sleeps in her bassinet

her tiny body

braving the dark alone

She is good when

she cries at a party

her angry wail interrupting

your good time

She is good when

she naps out at a dinner

her tiny palms

pressing against my chest

She is good when

she fills her diaper in public

her cute outfit

soiled in need of a soak

She is good when

she keeps her smocks clean

her sweet hair

pulled back with a bow

She is good when

she cries from hunger

she cries from tiredness

she cries for no reason at all

She is a baby

a small and innocent baby

so she is good

no matter what

iii.

i never knew
how much my body
could hold, grow, work, do
until there was you

c-section scars

To get to you, they <u>cut</u> through me.
Seven layers of tissue, muscles, me
all to bring you here.
I felt it all on that table, hands tied
telling myself, "just one more hour."
That's all that separated me from you.
An hour of surgery separated me
from you.
The tiny little smile of a scar is just
a token of my time, a small reminder
of the burning pain alive in my body
for weeks while I tried to care for you.
The mornings when your dad had to
raise me from the bed as I winced and
cried and thought it might break me to
hold you.
But I held you anyway, close, smiling.
The pain faded and the scar stayed and
I'll keep it forever to remind myself that
you and I are stronger than we knew.

if you are awake right now

If you are awake right now

with an upset, fussy baby

your eyes red and glossy

desperate to get back to sleep

Somewhere down the street

or somewhere across the world

Somewhere in a small apartment

or somewhere in an old house

there is a mother

just like you

A mother who prays for just

one more hour of rest before

the sun rises on another day

A mother who balances a

busy, blooming toddler alongside

her fresh new baby

A mother who feels alone

but also in desperate need of

her alone time

A mother who is doing this

for the very first time and

feels like she's ten steps behind

A mother who is living hour to hour

feed to feed, pump to pump

and short nap to short nap

If you are awake right now

with an upset, fussy baby

you are one of many mothers

reaching across miles and minutes

saying, "you are not alone."

iv.

stop telling moms

to "enjoy it now"

we are desperately

trying to soak up seconds

that are already gone

maternity leave

Hardly a vacation.
If so, 2/10 would not recommend.
The baby is cute but
the exhaustion is
less than luxurious.
Would bet big money
this "vacation" would break you
more than your corporate job
in your comfy office chair.
Want to compare?
Try these stitches on for size.
You'll want a peri bottle and
ice packs and disposable undies
for your troubles.
Who needs a tiny bikini and an
island breeze when you
have all these
postpartum amenities?
Lucky you.
Lucky, lucky you.

time is a thief

Time is a thief

Public Enemy Number One

tricker than the Joker

slicker than Bonnie & Clyde

Who can save us?

Is Batman on patrol?

Can Robin Hood steal from

the time-rich and give back to

the time-poor?

* * *

Don't blink

they say as if

my reddened, dry eyes

will see more

hold more

store more away

Time takes my baby from me

   Week by week

   Pound by pound

   Inch by inch

I see her grow in the shadows of

her outgrown clothes

her shedding naps

her discarded swaddles

Time is a thief

It steals from us all

blinking or sleeping

vigilant or weary

Time takes and takes

* * *

I have no platitude

no cliche words

to ease the discomfort

of passing days

But all I can say

is that I'm so damn grateful

to steal as many moments

with her as I'm able

Time may be a thief

but so is her mom

and I'm coming for it all

belle

Belle is the name we gave you

because *belle* is who you are

We spun you out of beauty

Gold braided from straw

And of all the names to suit you

Belle fit best of all

V.

you were made for

frolicks in fairy gardens

cheeks brushed by butterfly wings

a world of pure enchantment

my mother is magic

My mother carries fun in the palms of her hands. Sprinkling joy wherever she treads. Hours spent shopping for books at the library. Leisure mornings with markers on craft paper, easels stationed on the front porch. Dance recitals in the living room. *Watch me twirl, Mama!* We were the explorers. Taking to the woods and the water and returning to her with stories of our adventures. She carries fun still. Spontaneous trips to the beach. Last minute flights to Disney World. Ordinary Target runs transformed into silly, forever memories. My mother is magic. Pixie dust inhabited. How grateful I am to share my mother with you. How hopeful I am to be like her.

vi.

you take us

out into the world

everything is new

oh, what sights

there are to see

you look great, mama!

You look great, mama! You look like you slept ten straight hours last night and definitely were not waking up every hour on the hour. So refreshed. You look like you are losing the baby weight in a time that impresses us and makes us feel happy for you. Thank God, you don't actually look like you've given birth! You are bouncing back! You definitely don't look like you cried yesterday because you had to put away the newborn outfits. You're not even puffy! You look like you don't need any help and we like that. You look like you didn't have a baby at all! It's a miracle! If you didn't look "great" we would ask you, "are you okay?" with concern and a condescending head tilt.

But you're great, you're just so great!

vii.

one day

this will all feel

very far away

what a sad day

that will be

let me never forget

Your tiny, soft fingers curling around my thumb.

Your free little body relaxing in a warm bath.

The way your whole self reacts when I enter a room.

Oh, mama is here, it says.

Your gummy, magnetic smile giving way to your dimples.

How full and whole my arms feel with you in them.

The quieting of your cries at the sound of your favorite songs.

The crown of your head tucked beneath my chin.

Your balled-up fists stretching to the sky, greeting the day.

The smell of your wet hair or the smell of your dewy, moisturized skin.

You in every stage of yourself. Growing, learning, changing.

That we are each other's, forever and always.

viii.

some days

you feel like

my entire personality

but then I

remember that

I'm still me

someone's mother

She is someone's mother now. She, the girl who skinned her knees on the blacktop after class. She, the girl who cried in the corner of the gym over the boy who didn't ask her to dance. She, the girl who tanned her skin on sunny, sandy beaches. She, the girl with fashion choices she wishes she could unmake. Overalls at the roller rink. Gaucho pants at the football game. Peasant skirts and random graphic tees. She, the girl with the big life choices. The English degree or the medical school? The faraway city or the homegrown roots? She, the girl who married the boy who was so nice it scared her. She, the girl who threw coins in wishing wells. She is someone's mother now. And she is also still a someone. Life will start over again, she sometimes at the sidelines, she sometimes on the main stage. Interested and interesting. Dreaming and dreamed.

ix.

i'll hold you

for just a few

more minutes

and maybe

just a few

minutes more

mother feelings

I rethink my life. Positioning my lens over my own mother's eye. How big her mother feelings must have been, how big my mother feelings are now. She guides me into a kindergarten class. *You're going to have so much fun!* Does she cry when she gets to her car? Does she feel relief for gained time? She lets me go then. And again. And again. High school. College. First jobs in different states. *You're going to have so much fun!* She sets herself aside. Over and over. Holding back her big mother feelings so I can grow. So I can go. I'll do this, too. Guide my own girl to places I can't follow. Waiting to meet her the moment she needs me again.

an anxious mother

Are you an anxious person?

No, not really

Are you an anxious mother?

Well.

It's just that I don't know why
she's crying right now and
I don't know if she's ever
going to actually sleep and I'm
not sure if she's getting
enough tummy time or maybe
I'm letting her nap for too long or
maybe not at the right times of day
and I know I should be following
these schedules in these books

but my baby doesn't want to nap
at 11:00 a.m. exactly and also I
don't want her to cry it out and
feel like no one is coming to save
her because the world is going to
be hard enough and shouldn't she
at least know for now that someone
will be there to catch her because
one day she will be a teenage girl
and the world is a hard, mean, cold
place for teenage girls and maybe
if I just pick her up now it will create
a subconscious ripple effect into her
life and if that's true then what if it's
also true about the bad events like
that time I put her in a onesie that
was too tight and I didn't realize how
uncomfortable she was and maybe
she will hold that over me in some way
forever?

Are you an anxious mother?
Who isn't?

X.

is there a

joy as great

as when your

eyes find mine?

club baby

We used to dance close
in hot, sweaty bars
plastic cups sloshing in our hands
to lyrics about
hips that do not lie
romances that go bad
cities that we run tonight

Now we dance big
on soft, fluffy rugs
a little baby smiling wide up at us
to lyrics about
wheels on buses
purple monkeys in bubblegum trees
and rainbow connections

xi.

bless this body
that broke open
to make way
for you

bounce back

I have no need
to bounce back.
To look, to live, to be
the person I once was
before I was a mother.
Let me honor the body
that brought us together.
Let me allow this vessel
to end its wrestle
forcing itself smaller, thinner.
Instead I can let it rest
knowing it's done glorious things.
I will ask nothing of it.
It can wear and be and exist
in whatever size it requires.
I will simply offer a thank you
and a kind supportive hug.
I have no desire for backwards.
Only forward. Anew.

the world i want to show you

I can't wait to share with you the world as I've seen it. Happy and worthwhile and beautiful things. A day full of baking with Mimi, brownie batter on a spoon, the smell of fresh-baked cookies filling a room. Holiday traditions, caravans to the Christmas tree farm, parmesan squares on a Thanksgiving day. I want to show you beauty up close. Sunsets on a Florida beach, a spring flush of Old Garden Roses, an evening walk in the woods. I'll show you the experiences I return to over and over. A musical performance on a Broadway stage, a good book by the pool, a firework show over Cinderella's Castle. And as you grow, you'll find your own happy and worthwhile and beautiful things. I can't wait for you to share with me the world as you see it.

actually, i can wait

On second thought, allow me to hit pause. To count the eyelashes that brush against your brow. To hook my finger in the tiny dimple behind your knee. To bring your plump cheek to mine. To dress you in a fancy outfit you'll soon outgrow. I can wait for you to find sleep in your crib, in a room of your own, instead of nestled beside me in your bassinet. I can wait for the first holidays with you. The first family trips. I will happily wait for the first time I hear you say my name. I can wait for tomorrow and even tonight. I'll spend my time in the moment with you, holding you close, wanting to *pause, pause, pause.*

xii.

i love you

i love you

i love you

and oh did

i mention

i love you?

my husband is a father now

My husband is a father now.
Assembler of baby toys.
Fumbler of snaps and buttons
on tiny girl dresses.
The man that I married is now
the man that will raise her.
I chose him carefully.
Picked him, a shiny diamond
from a dense gravel driveway.
A road that led us to her.

He used to be mine, and I his.
Now we are both hers.
Our time together dwindles but
we make memories from minutes.
Slow dancing beside a stack of
dirty dishes, baby in her bouncer.
Long hugs in the hallway as we
hand off our girl.
I miss him from across the house.
But week by week, little by little,
we belong to each other again.

xiii.

can i go with you?

together

you and me

is just as it is

meant to be

firsts and lasts

Motherhood deals in a currency

of firsts and lasts

We exchange our endings for

new beginnings

Life taking from our pocketbooks

without asking

I give up a last newborn scrunch

for a first giggle

I spend my money and I'll go all in

all to witness you

xiv.

i never knew love

could feel so bright

the kind that blinds

and consumes

a yellow highlighter

a summer sun at noon

that's the love

I feel for you

i miss this already

I miss you in advance

This little version of you

The one sleeping on my chest

as I type this over your shoulder

This little version of you

who needs me so and holds me

closer than close

I miss you yesterday and

the day before that

Five pounds ago as well as

five weeks ago, so fast

it flew right by me

I'll miss this moment of you too

I already do

sisters

I hope you'll be a sister

with a sibling to call your own

Someone to tattle on

Someone to scheme with

Someone to share it all

I imagine you with a sister

because a sister is all I've known

Curling irons on the bathroom sink

Playing dress up and pretend

Hours sharing stories on the phone

* * *

I hope you'll be a sister

as great a sibling as my own

Someone to share your life with

Someone to cheer you on

Someone to call home

And if you never have a sister

I'll gift you with mine

She loves you almost as much as I do

The best of all time

XV.

heaven is your

little head

nestled into me

boring is beautiful

Boring is the most beautiful state. Saltine crackers on a beige dinner plate. White gel manicures. Checking your inbox. Checking it again. Loads of laundry all over the place: chaos in a hamper, folded on the coffee table, dirty, dirtier. Paying bills. Paying bills again. Waking up to your husband's freight-train-snores. Waking up to your baby's hunger cries. Feeding your baby. Feeding her again. Feeding her every two hours every day every week. Diaper changes. More diaper changes. It's all too fragile and all too fleeting. It's all so boring and all so beautiful. Aren't we the luckiest?

xvi.

i tell myself

i'm doing a good job

and i hope one day

you'll echo that back

to me too

she looks just like you!

I know you mean she has my eyes but
I want you to mean she looks like
someone who has faced
hard things, sad stories, discomfort
and became better for it.
I want you to mean she looks like
someone who isn't always
sure that she loves her body but
wears jean shorts anyway.
I hope that she looks like
someone who cries at dog videos,
reads the news and takes action,
someone who trusts her intuition.
I love that she has my eyes but at the
end of the day
I pray they will be
the least important features
she inherits from me.

xvii.

the first time
i saw you
i knew you
deep down
to my soul

nine months
of just us
and then
you were here
in my arms

heartbeat to
heartbeat
body to body
just like
we always were

everything changes

Stormy weather clears for
sunny, warm skies.
The coffee always cools.
But I will always love you.

Quiet mornings fade into
busy, crowded afternoons.
Tires go flat.
But I will always love you.

Crisp, dead leaves fall
as the temperature drops.
Friends lose touch.
But I will always love you.

My love for you grows
every hour of every day.
It changes and swells.
I will always love you.

i wish you were here to meet her

I wish you were here to meet her

to see what your granddaughter made.

I know what you'd say and I can

hear how you'd say it.

"Jenny, look at all her hair!"

Excited. Animated. Awed.

I wish you were here to meet her

but I know that you were ready to go.

I could hear it in your phone calls.

I could see it on your face.

You told me you would wait for her

and you were a woman of your word.

I wish you were here to meet her
to teach her all that you've taught me.
The importance of a good book.
The beauty of a Van Gogh.
I will do my best to teach her all the
lessons that you shared with me.

I wish you were here to meet her
but maybe you already did.
Maybe you crossed paths in the
Heavenly hallway, you stepping out
as she made her way in

my heart is a person now

My heart is a person now.
She breathes and giggles and
finds the world to be a
magical, beautiful place.

My heart is a person now.
And the body she left behind
worries and hurries and
prays that nothing bad will
try and find her.

My heart is a person now.
What a miracle she is.

what i'd give up

Empty arms. The convenience of "just running to the store real quick." My pretty, pregnancy hair. Lazy Sunday mornings. Relaxing, in general. A pre-childbirth body. Red stretch marks across my pale skin. A kangaroo pouch where you used to live. Sleep, in all its forms. Nights, mornings, 2 a.m. and 2:10 a.m. and 2:16 a.m. Alcohol. Sushi date nights. Manicures. Leisurely getting ready, curling my hair, looking up makeup tutorials. Spontaneously booking airfare. Spending money without thinking too hard. I'd give all this up for you and so much more, baby of mine.

big family

You will never know

a life without cousins

who beg to play with you

Uncles and aunts

who fight to hold you

Holidays with loud voices

Family vacations

Big tables for birthday dinners

You'll have love

for your whole life

Traditions you treasure

Celebrations you'll

always remember

This is my favorite
gift that I can give you
A lasting tree of loving
family members and
memories you'll get to
keep forever

we grow together

We grow together

My body expands

while yours forms

connected and

dependent

We grow together

I learn motherhood

while you learn

personhood

trialing and

erroring

We grow together

I try to relax

while you try to

experience

exploring and

observing

We grow together

I become new

while you do

too

living and

letting live

xviii.

watch me

tend to your dreams

like tomatoes on a vine

tender and fruitful

as carefully as they were mine

i dreamed new dreams

I dreamed of Broadway stages
curtain calls for standing ovations
belting ballads under deep blue lights
my name on the marquee

but the Great White Way
was not my destiny

I dream new dreams
solo shows and a cappella melodies
A tiny audience of one
staring back up at me

I'll bring Broadway to you
my favorite audience, your mom's debut

xix.

i measured your life in days

then tracked you by weeks

we snapped your monthly photos

and one day time will pass in years

and I'll think back to when you

were just a few minutes old

mom guilt (baby edition)

The immediate need to apologize for not being everything and knowing everything and doing everything. *I'm sorry, I'm new at this. I'm sorry my house is a mess.* To lead with excuses to make our decisions more palatable. *No, I didn't breastfeed because. No, I didn't take 12 weeks off because. No, I don't want any more children because.* I'm too much. *Can you wash your hands? Sorry, germaphobe!* I'm not enough. *I thought I would be better at this.* I'm messing everything up. *I effed up her nap schedule. I shrunk her clothes. The bath water is too cold.* I exist with a constant pit in my stomach that every choice I make is setting you up to resent me, fodder for your future therapist, blemishes I cannot correct. But then I hold you. Curl your body into mine. And the guilt noise quiets, making room for joy.

father figures

As much as a daughter
needs a mother
The world needs girls
with good fathers

I'm the daughter of a man
who wasn't afraid to sit down
and play a round
of Barbies with me

I'm the daughter of a man
who ran and swam and cycled
in triathlons
I watched him sweat and grind
and cross finish lines

I'm the daughter of a man
with a new heart
A healthy man dealt a bad hand
that led to a sickness
and a miracle cure

You are the daughter of the
daughter of a good father

You are this man's granddaughter
He built you a nursery and
holds you while I work
He gives puppet shows
and knows about tummy time

You are also the daughter of
a good father

You are the daughter of a man
who buys flowers on his way home
from a long day of work
carefully tending to them
in their vases

You are the daughter of a man
who pays attention
to every person in the room
starting conversations with the one
who doesn't seem to know anyone

You are the daughter of a man
who loves you more than
he could ever have imagined
Late nights rocking you to sleep
Mornings excited to see your smile

I watch these men adore you
strong and sensitive men I love
come to love you too
your father and mine

Here's to the daughters
and here's to their fathers
Good men aren't always
so hard to find

unoriginal

Can you believe it? She grabbed her toes today! She is a prodigy, a genius, a marvel! She is the first baby in the entire world to grab her own toes. She is the first baby in the entire world to exist, to breathe, to suck, to smile, to be. And I am the first mother. I am the first to carry her, kiss her, feed her, know her. Oh, how unoriginal it all is. Oh, how mother after mother has blazed a trail of tears, wounds, and swollen love. I'll walk behind you, grateful, knowing the ones behind me hold their babies close thinking they too are the only ones in the universe.

XX.

i wish to approach

the world

with as much delight

as my baby discovering

her own toes

i keep you

I keep you fed
I keep you clean
I keep you soothed
I keep you rested
I keep you warm
I keep you comfortable
I keep you safe
I keep you clothed
I keep you healthy
I keep you close
but
I can't keep you little
I can't keep you safe
I can't keep you happy
I can't keep you painless
I can't keep you whole
I can't keep you innocent
I can't keep you

xxi.

she falls asleep

and I stare at her picture

wondering how

i could miss her

from just a few feet away

sensations

I lose the sensations like sand through my grip. The way it felt to exist with you inside. The weight of it. A few months ago but it's lost to me already. The feel of my rounded belly. The flutter of your kick. The waddling way I moved from room to room. And then you were here. So small and new. But that's gone too. How did it feel to hold the initial seven pounds of you? You're double that now. You move and you reach and you grow every day. And the feeling of you in my arms fades away. I'll take the pictures and the videos, knowing that I fight a losing battle. All the images won't resurrect the warmth of your tiny fingers on the skin of my neck. But I try anyway. The sand slips through.

fur baby

When I needed someone to love
I found you
The sweetest of the litter
mine from the moment we met

For a while it was just us two
learning tricks, couch cuddles
baths in the kitchen sink
playing ball in a tiny city yard

Your dad found us next
and you had a new playmate
He fit right into our little family
our missing piece

But there was still always
just me and you

When I was pregnant
I thought for sure you'd know
But you didn't seemed to notice
as you saw my stomach grow

Now you have a sister
A brand new person to love
You keep us close to you
sitting vigil in our sleepless nights

And while our lives look different
and there's less time for us to play
I'll never forget to make time for you
small moments in every day

Because there will always be time
for just me and you

xxii.

you are the mark

i want to make

you are the chance

i got to take

legacy

I feel the urgent need
to create a legacy
as a woman with a dream

So you can watch me
set a goal
and work to succeed

Big, bold ideas
like bestseller lists and
travels to faraway places

I'll take you with me
my little shadow
your own dreams await

nights

Good evening, little one.

I run your bath water.

Grab your animal hooded towel.

You kick your legs; water splashes.

I sing you love songs.

Soapy washcloths on soft baby skin.

I pick you up, wrap you dry and warm.

Heavy eyelids and stretchy, sleepy hands.

I swaddle you.

Nights were never quite
as good before there was you.

also by jenny bravo

These Are The Moments: A Novel

Those Were the Days: A Short Story

That Was The Year: A Novel

Take Me Home for Christmas: A Novella

Good News of Great Joy: Christmas Poetry

acknowledgments

I feel like I need to equally thank the following people for helping me write this book and also helping me on my motherhood journey. I hope I honored all of you in my writing. And I hope you all know how much you mean to me.

- **Kyle**. I love you x 1,000,000. Thank you for being the best partner, father, husband, and friend. Thank you for keeping our house clean. Thank you for every peanut butter and jelly sandwich. Thank you for all of it. You're even better than I imagined you would be.
- **Mom**. Thank you for setting an incredible example of motherhood. For being my best friend. For taking a late night shift when I was in desperate need of it. For mothering me even now. For taking on a whole new way of life to help me with Belle while I work. What a gift you are.
- **Dad**. It is not lost on me how grateful I need to be to have you here with me and my girl. Thank you for holding Belle while she naps. Thank you for teaching her (and me) about the beauty in nature all around us. We love you immensely.
- **Monica**. We'd be lost without Honey. Thank you for taking a week off to be with me and my newborn baby. Thank you for taking care of us always. Thank you for cooking for us and capturing incredible photos of our family. You always show up.

- **Mere. (And Lou).** I miss you both so much and think about you every day. It makes me happy to know you're together again.
- **Ms. Gail/Queenie.** I lucked out in the mother-in-law department. Thank you for all you do for us. For the most incredible nursery and the memories that come with it. I love watching how Belle lights up when she sees you. Thank you for raising Kyle to be the man that he is.
- **Blair, Bonnie, Courtney, Elise, Kathryn.** I would not know half the motherhood "tips and tricks" that I know without you. Thank you for always being there to answer my questions, to support me through the hard times and celebrate with me in the good times. Like the first time she slept 2 hours at one time.
- **Tina, Matthew, Austin, and Caroline.** Aka T, Activity Matt, Charlesy, and Goose. You four know what you mean to me. Watching you with Belle feels like coming full circle. I love how much you love her. Thank you for always being there.
- **Charles/Habibi.** I'm so grateful for a brother-in-law like you. Thank you for being a safe place and always offering words of encouragement.
- **Nicole.** Thank you for reading these poems and giving me courage to publish them. You and KK are more like sisters than friends to me and I'm honored to be your honorary big sister.
- **Belle's big families.** To my aunts and uncles and cousins, I have always been so proud to be part of this big, beautiful family. Thank you for loving my girl the way that you do. For always saying yes to a party. For all the years of holidays and birthdays and traditions. I can't wait to continue our fun with her. To the big family that I married into, thank you for welcoming me in with open arms. You feel like an extension of home and I'm so glad Belle gets to have you.

about the author

Jenny Bravo is an author and poet who lives in Covington, Louisiana with her husband, daughter, and dog who is more like a son. She published her first book, *These Are the Moments,* in 2015 after blogging her writing process. You can stay in touch with her on Instagram, TikTok, and her newsletter.

www.ingramcontent.com/pod-product-compliance
Lightning Source LLC
Chambersburg PA
CBHW070437010526
44118CB00014B/2088